ZenLux

Architecture and Electronics

 GALLUP

Duncan Brown

SITES/Lumen Books
40 Camino Cielo
Santa Fe, New Mexico 87501
(505) 988-9236

© 1996 Lumen, Inc.
ISBN: 0-930829-39-5
Printed in the United States of America

SITES/Lumen Books are produced by Lumen, Inc., a tax-exempt, non-profit organization.
Lumen, Inc. is supported, in part, with public funds from the National Endowment for the
Arts as well as with private contributions.

CONTENTS

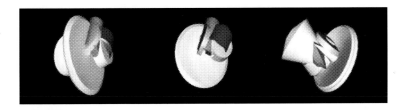

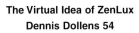

Juan Gris, *Breakfast*, 1914
Cut-and-pasted paper,
crayon, and oil over canvas,
31 7/8 X 23 1/2 inches.
Collection, The Museum of
Modern Art, New York.
Acquired through the
Lillie P. Bliss Bequest.

The work presented here is a selection of projects related to the computer transformation of Juan Gris's 1914 painting *Breakfast* and its application to architecture. The projects track the development through simple transformations, environments in a graphic novel, programmed buildings, rapid prototyping models, and virtual reality experiments on the Web.

The painting, initially a relatively arbitrary selection, was appropriated to reinvigorate current spatial conceptions. Selected forms within the painting were projected, folded, and spun to generate new structures, which in turn underwent further translation, gradually moving away from their origin in an affirmative play. The computer worked as an active tool in this endeavor, allowing creation of conceptually complex orders and their dynamic representation from multiple viewpoints.

Beyond design exploration and production, the computer is increasingly involved in social communication and exchange as well as in spatial conceptualization. Reflecting Virilio's comment that from now on "architecture is only a movie," the graphic novel *DuneRay* combines the drawn-in architecture with the element of time in film. In *DuneRay*, the different computer models are used in various combinations and scales to create fields and environments. These environments become the location for frame sequences simulating scene structures from movies and comic books. The frames are combined in a form of temporal collage: the storyboard for a nonlinear, non-narrative, silent movie.

Subsequent to *DuneRay*, a number of projects and competitions were undertaken to translate the techniques and models to programmed space and buildings. Under the auspices of a fictitious cyber real estate company, ZenLux, form was tested against function. Typically, the painting is used to generate a spatial structure that is then inhabited—for example, the 14th Street Mall. In the case of the Scottish Design Center, program and context led to a diagram into which model types were inserted. The diagram in turn was modified and a reiterative loop developed enriching the design process.

4

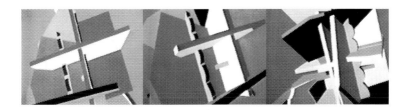

Computer applications are already well established in the production side of construction; however, the new tools are simply layered over the traditional techniques of spatial management and control. Rather than simply continue to produce "drawings," there is an opportunity for a radical synthesis of the real and digital realms.

There is a shift between traditional architectural representation and computer modeling—what is created on screen is the end result. At a small scale, the equipment for this sort of manufacture already exists, and, as with plastic model kits, it is not hard to imagine entire buildings fabricated from cast component parts.

Being an architect online, I am particularly interested in efforts to create a virtual reality language that can be utilized on the World Wide Web. Away from the power of Silicon Graphics and Hollywood software, the game *Doom* offers a glimpse of the future of Web space. *Doom* involves travel through a real three-dimensional environment and the possibility for up to four players to experience the space interactively.

Numerous shareware editors have appeared on the Net, allowing people to edit and create their own spaces or levels. I envisage an architectural studio in the future where something like DoomCad will replace AutoCad and environments will be created interactively as people link levels and spaces to one another. With the recent arrival of VRML browsers and builders, the ZenLux Web site is just beginning to explore real three-dimensions on the Web.

The strategies outlined above are considered a commitment, as Andrew Ross says, "to making our knowledge about technoculture into something like a hacker's knowledge, capable of penetrating existing systems of rationality that might otherwise be seen as infallible; a hacker's knowledge, capable of reskilling and, therefore, of rewriting the cultural programs and reprogramming the social values that make room for new technologies."

OPERATIONS

Transformation Sequence

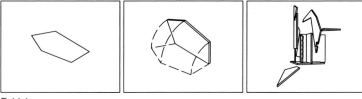

Projection

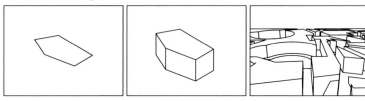

Fold-1

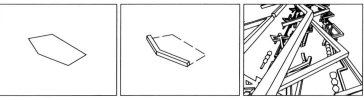

Profile

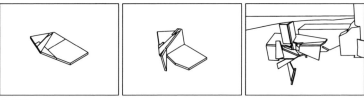

Fold-2

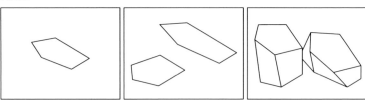

Asymmetrical Projection

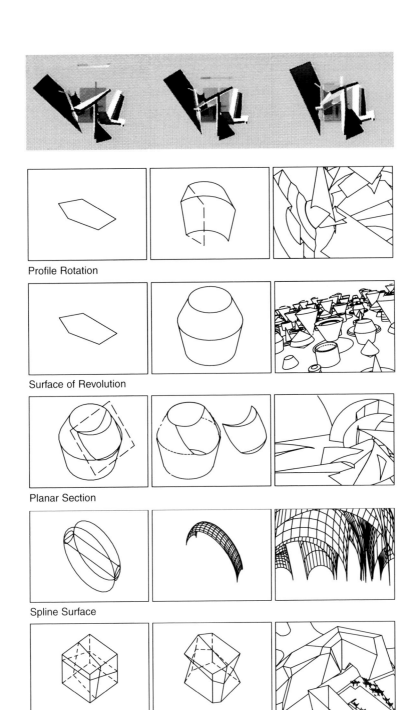

Profile Rotation

Surface of Revolution

Planar Section

Spline Surface

Scaled Surface

DUNERAY

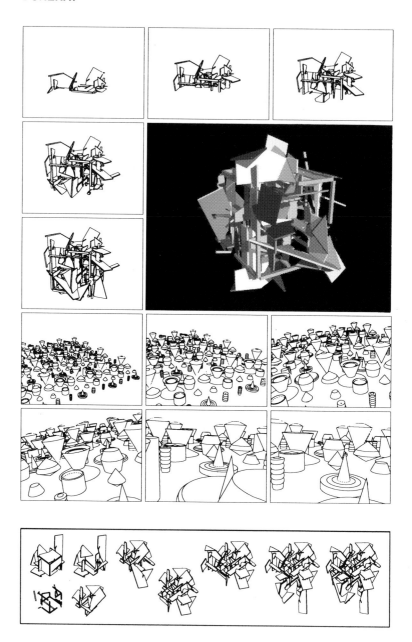

DuneRay—Plate 1
Nest 8—Generation Sequence

8

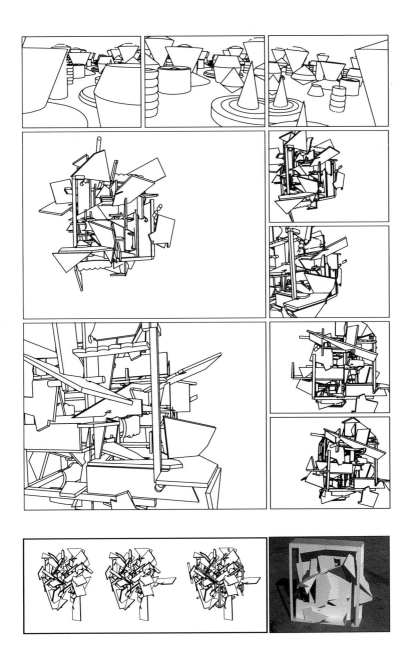

DuneRay—Plate 2
Coupled—Model

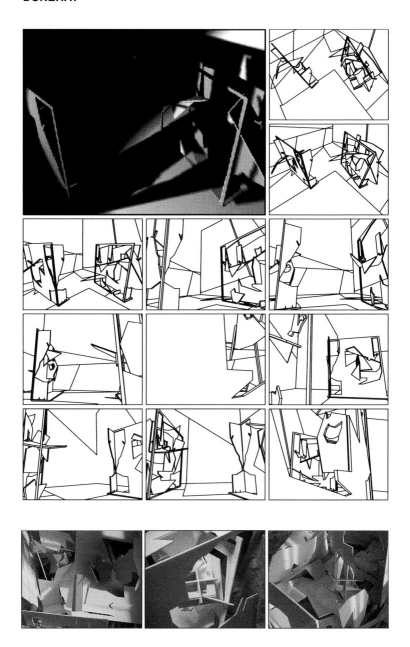

DuneRay—Plate 33
Discoupled—Model

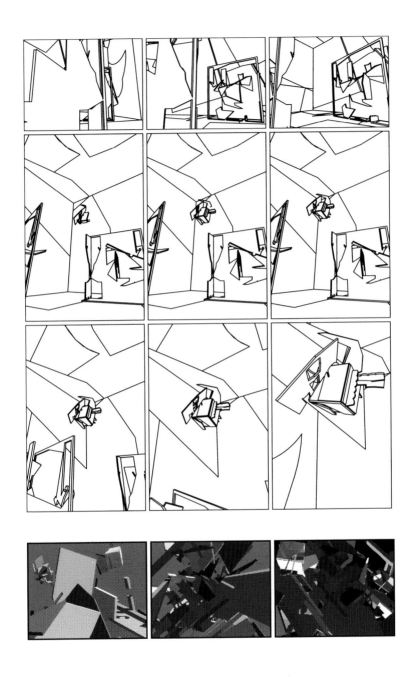

DuneRay—Plate 34
Sites 2, 4 & 5—Raytraces

ZENLUX ESTATES

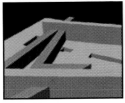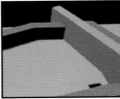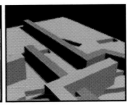

Amid the scandal and corruption of its final days, the administration passed legislation halting all new construction for one hundred years. In an attempt to forestall total urban decay and the further exhaustion of natural resources, the government mandated a shift in focus to the rehabilitation and reuse of existing building stock coupled with the development of applications for reconstituted building materials.

While initial reaction was one of dismay, ultimately this gave way to a very healthy and vigorous growth in the building industry, as creative programming revitalized urban centers. Old centers thrived as opposed to simply being nodes or data-drops; underoccupied office spaces were converted to apartment buildings, abandoned warehouses to administrative offices, old schools to museums, many buildings found new use by housing a combination of programs.

The role of the architect all but disappeared as the corporatization of the construction company sublimated the activity to that of another technical department within the industry. All that remained, as had been forecast by the rise of the "culture of architecture" in the nineties, was an aesthetic, almost anthropological interest in the cultural representation of historic spatial structures. In this postprofessional environment, architects found work within the construction companies in an expanded but less defined role as construction technocrats, went "back to the land" as community builders (Alexandrians), or became "celebrity" architects on the Internet.

The shift from new construction also led to the development of a virtual real estate—ZenLux being one of these. ZenLux was basically founded on the remains of Microsoft with investment from a Chinese bioware manufacturer. Initially located in the Manhattan 1960s landmark, the NetLife building, but moving later to an upstate campus, ZenLux grew quickly to market domination.

In developing the field of construction animation and robotics, new spatial models for housing and offices were generated for the period beyond the construction moratorium, and these acquired a speculative value. So much so that in the interests of security these estates were developed and maintained by a constantly moving cadre of engineers (databoys), accessing the database from transient and remote locations.

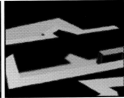

Above—ZenLux Estates screenshades
Opposite—ZenLux Estates Site Plan

15

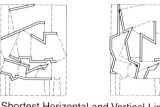

Shortest Horizontal and Vertical Lines
Through the Painting

Horizontal and Vertical Projections

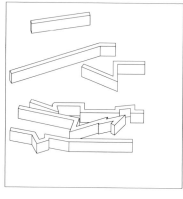

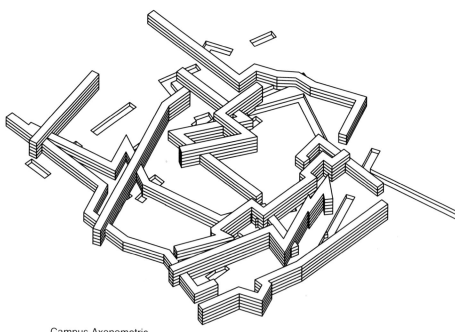

Campus Axonometric
Opposite—Model Photographs

16

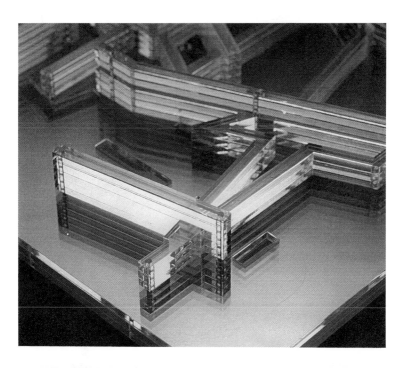

FOURTEENTH STREET MALL

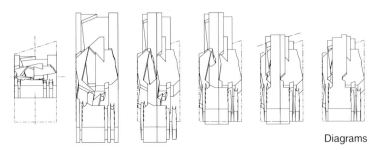

Diagrams

The 14th Street Mall utilizes a block at 14th and Broadway in Manhattan. Half the block was vacant, and the other half was occupied by a large apartment building, the Palladium, some small shops, and housing. Developing the notion of projecting the painting forms volumetrically, the painting is scaled onto the site. Previous investigations generated schemes with relatively simple sections. Fourteenth Street Mall moves this a little further. Instead of being projected from a ground-zero base line, section profiles are developed around a horizontal datum—fixed above ground. A logic of maneuvers develops in relation to the site. The framing perimeter forms are shifted to the center, anchoring as opposed to enframing the forms contained within. Interest in a linear building led to extending the building beyond the site and to then collapse it back in, creating overlapping volumes in the east-west direction.

To further develop the massing of the building, lines from the painting are layered over the building volumes. Layers carrying information about transparency are applied to the volumes, based on their sectional hierarchy and function. In determining a program for the building, the existing facilities were redistributed on the site. The retail and nightclub were combined to create a twenty-four-hour mall. A large indoor public space strengthens and extends 14th Street. The housing is distributed horizontally along the south side of the site, and parking is below grade.

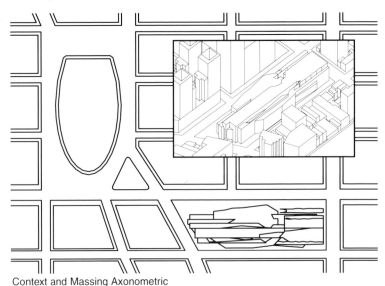

Context and Massing Axonometric

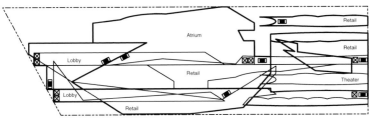

Ground Floor

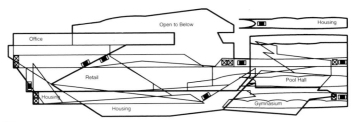

Third Floor

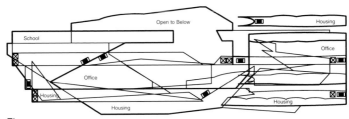

Sixth Floor

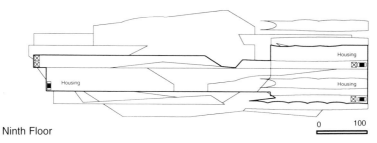

Ninth Floor

0   100

Massing models

21

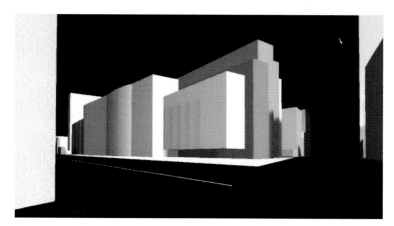

View at Fourteenth Street and Fourth Avenue

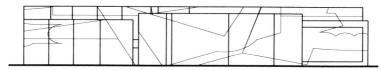

North Elevation

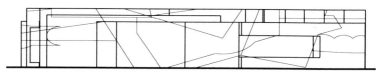

South Elevation

East and West Elevations

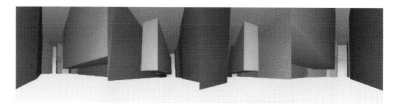

Atrium Interior Massing. Opposite—Section Slice

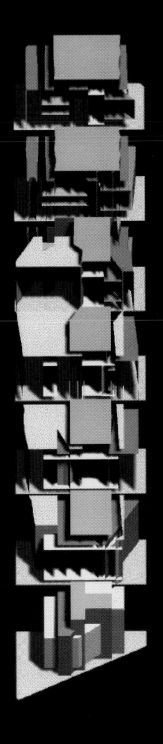

IRVING PLACE APARTMENT

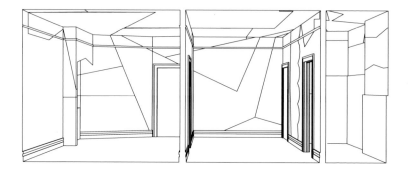

The Irving Place apartment continues a series of spatial experiments begun in other apartments. Located at 17th Street and Irving Place, Manhattan, in a prewar rental apartment building, the apartment is about 375 square feet, has a living room, kitchen alcove and bedroom, 10'-ceilings, and picture rail and heavy door moldings.

Using the computer, the painting is folded into a box and translated to the apartment walls in four colors. This allows a reinterpretation of the apartment volume. With allusions to van Doesburg's Cafe d'Aubette and Lizzitsky's Proun Room, the painted planes start to structure and define their own independent logic of space.

The full box fills the perimeter of the apartment while the residual portions of the net act as planes set into the box. The picture rail acts as a datum for the ceiling plane. A reading of a box with inserted planes is clear, looking through the doorway from the bedroom to the living room. Modeling the design on the computer establishes an experiential feedback loop between the real and the virtual.

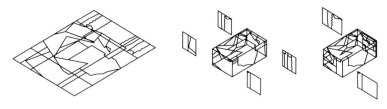

Diagrams

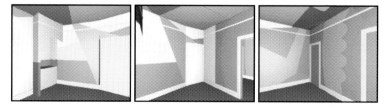

Apartment screenshades. Overleaf—Interior views. Nest 5 animation.

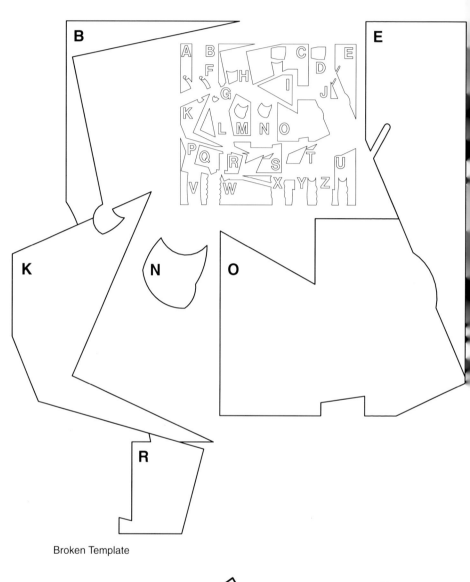

Broken Template

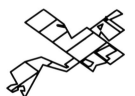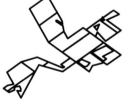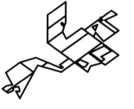

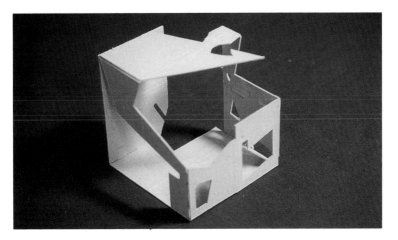

Broken—a condition described in space. Broken/Fixed—relative terms.
Having created spatial environments in previous apartments by spelling out words in space with string, I applied this principle to the painting and the Irving Place apartment. Each letter of the alphabet was assigned to a form within the painting, and the painting was folded in box form.

   Various words and phrases were then tried out in sketch and model form, moving back and forth between paper and digital space. Numerous small maquettes were created as pairs: one representing the word, the other residual form, the letters left over. These were introduced into the apartment as two cubes, one in each of the large rooms. Another layer of the painting nested within the painted space.

   After going through my name as well as the words *Architecture*, *Building*, and suchlike, *Broken* was selected. *Broken* because of the physical form of space generated, but for other reasons, too. *Broken* from the phrase "broken ladder" in Wenders' *Until the End of the World*. *Broken* from the Nine Inch Nails album. *Broken* from the misspelling of my surname on a Silicon Graphics World mailing list. *Broken free* . . .

   While originally conceived for a 4'x 8' plywood module, *Broken* was realized, because of economy, with large sheets of corrugated card. Where painting forms overlap one another, both are shown in outline, creating a filigree as opposed to a solid plane. Further experiments were suggested, as some of the models collapsed in under their own weight and took up profiles in tension. Or back in the electronic realm, filigree was layered within filigree.

Broken Fold

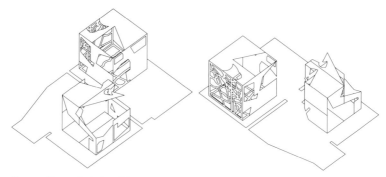

Broken Boxes in Irving Place apartment

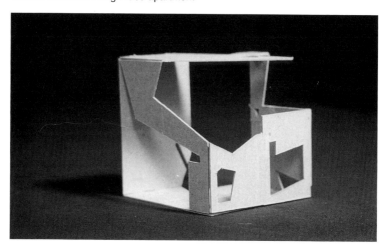

Broken model

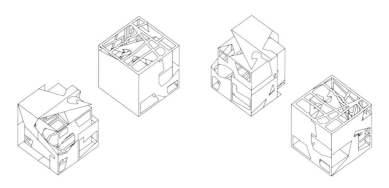

Broken Nested

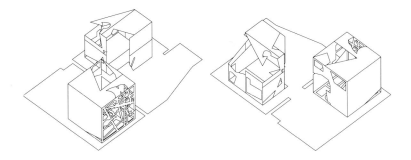

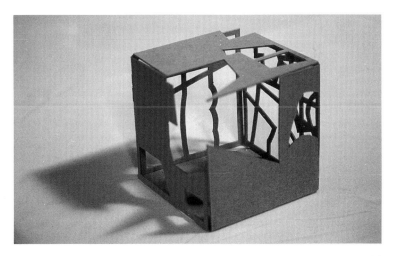

Broken model

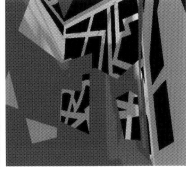

Broken Nested screenshades

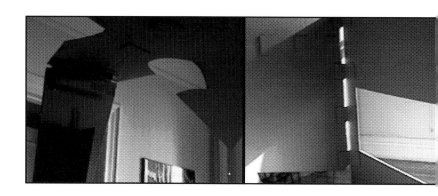

Broken Installation, February 1996

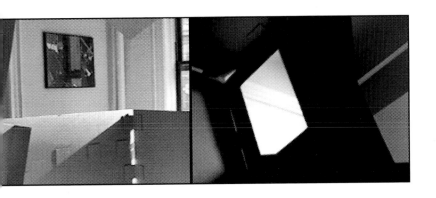

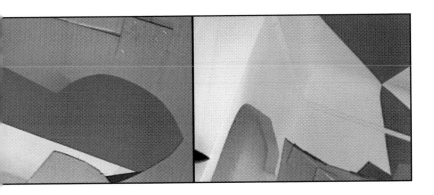

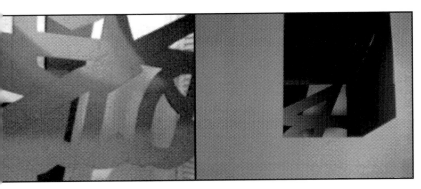

Video snapshots

RAPID PROTOTYPING

The architectural profession is only just beginning to address the implications of the new information society. Developments in the aerospace industry and multi-media communications have the potential to radically redefine the construction industry. Rapid prototyping allows for advance review of feasiblity and functionality of complex designs.

The Cubital process is one of the rapid prototyping techniques that translates three-dimensional CAD data, electronic form, into real objects. Cubital software slices CAD models into layers fractions of an inch thick. Then, as with a Xerox machine, an electrostatisized area of resin is solidified under ultraviolet light. The hardened resin is supported by a wax base and the process is repeated. The thin resin layers are fused together and, once the model is complete, the wax base is drained off.

The models depicted here are three tests using the Cubital process. The first was a simple volumetric study, which, since I was planning to visit friends in the area, also became a pretext for a visit to the plant in Toledo. The second model was a little more complicated: six sides of a box with cutouts held together by clip angles that had been placed in the design file. The third file was created from sections of rotated volumes, part of a study related to the computer manipulation of a Cubist painting.

While currently limited in size to 20" x 14" x 20", Cubital's potential for the construction industry is enormous. In the future, actual building components could be generated in a factory and then assembled on site. With developments of resins and fusing techniques, variations in color and transparency along with weatherproofing could be achieved. The challenge is to respond to these emergent protoyping technologies and assimilate them within architectural practice while reinforcing issues of design and quality of life.

Below—Hxa12, Stereolithography Model
Opposite—Lightbox Diagrams, and Stereolithography Model

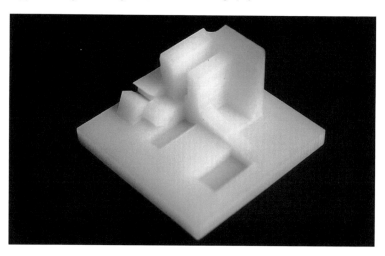

LIGHTBOX

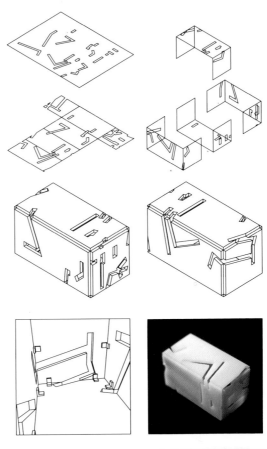

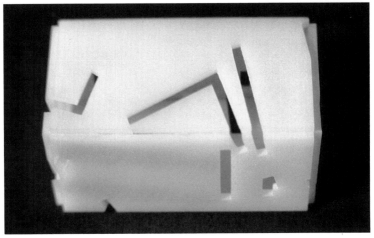

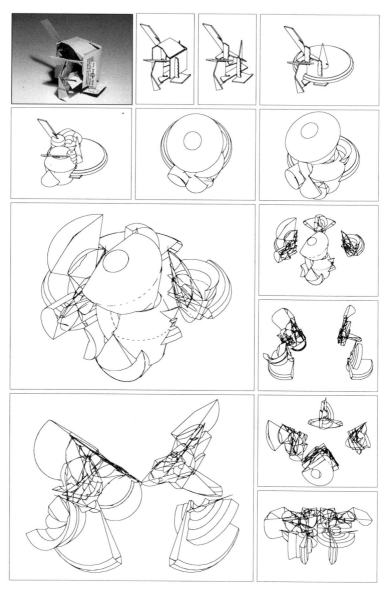

Transformation Sequence—
Nest #5's cubic armature is removed, leaving an assembly of free-floating planes.
The planes are rotated about their major axis to create a surface of revolution.
The volumes were then sliced into quadrants and a cast taken from one of the segments.
Opposite—Animation Sequence, and Stereolithography Model

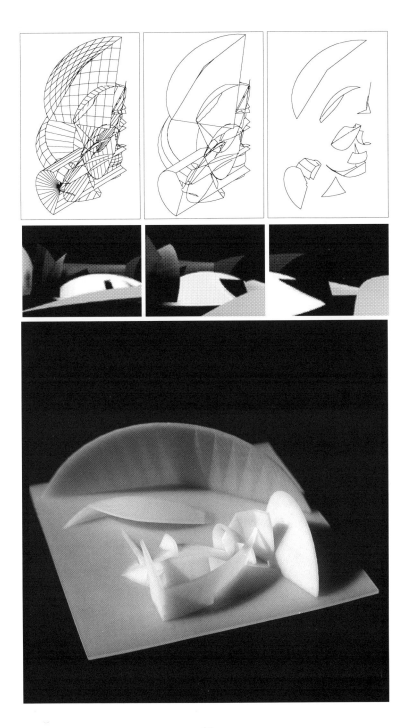

THE SCOTTISH ARCHITECTURE AND DESIGN CENTER

Having established a functional zoning for the Scottish Architecture and Design Center site, I introduced three type models from the painting—representative of three geometric orders. The models underwent further transformation relative to each other, as well as in response to general programmatic and contextual influences.

Like the volcanic rock that structures the rest of the city, the office component of the brief is separated into two large crystalline bars to create a dynamic figural space. The edge formed provides a backdrop for the Plaza, Design Center, and IMAX. In a traditional manner the plaza is completed with mature trees that establish a connection across the roadway and along Morrison Street to the Conference Center. A close between the Center and office buildings allows pedestrian access to Haymarket Station.

Sandstone-clad walls and stainless-steel roofing establish a continuity with the surrounding buildings and the city as a whole. The on-site parking is envisaged as a landscaped garden, which, with the increased use of public transportation, would gradually be returned to nature.

Elegantly curving concrete shell roofs give character to the Scottish Architecture and Design Center and house the exhibit spaces on the third and top floor. The ground floor is clad in sandstone, forming a solid base to the upper stories. This cladding gives way to a more open, glazed expression on the second floor and to the arcing vaults of the exhibit spaces on the third.

The large sandstone-clad drum of the Edinburgh IMAX acts as a marker for the entrance to the city from the west and anchors the complex to the southwest corner of the site. An electronic sign wraps the lower part of the base, and a large planar billboard advertises activities and events.

The commercial aspect of the brief is satisfied by two six-story office buildings. The two buildings average an area of 1350 square meters respectively per floor. The offices are clad in a sandstone wall panel, with punched operable openings at modular intervals in the faceted wall planes.

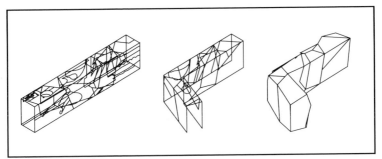

Office building

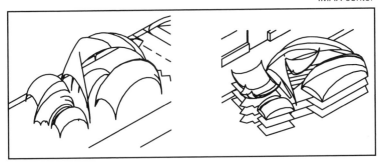

IMAX center

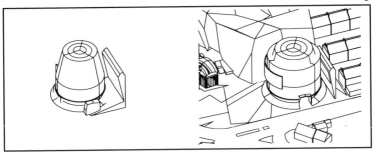

Design Center

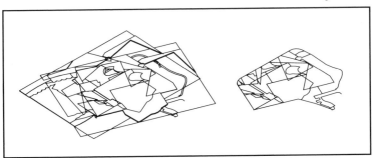

Site

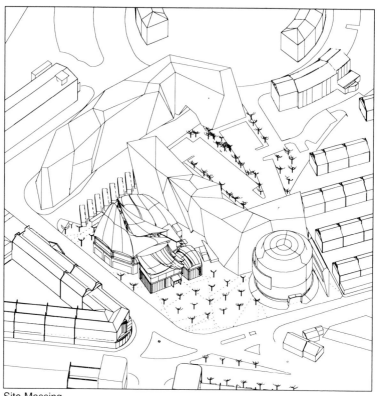

Site Massing
Haymarket Corner

Site Vignettes

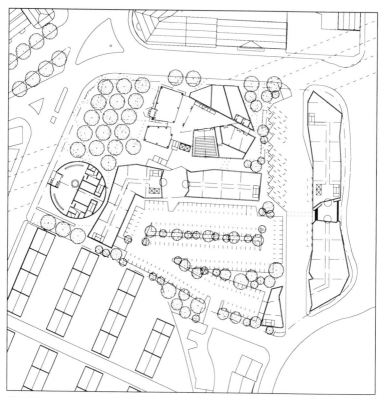

Site Plan

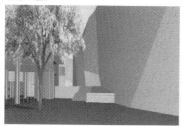

The Close between Office and Center

The Entrance Foyer

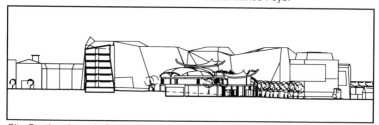

Site Section through Center looking South

**Design Center
Ground Floor**

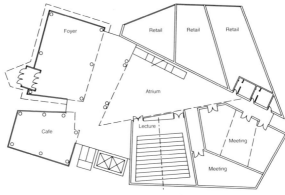

Foyer

Retail Retail Retail

Atrium

Cafe

Lecture

Meeting

Meeting

**Design Center
Library Floor**

Library

Studios

Open to Below

Education

Library

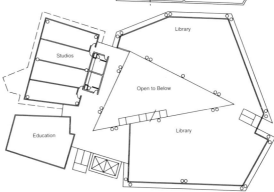

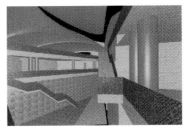

From the Atrium towards the Foyer   From the Library into the Atrium

Site Section through IMAX looking North

DOOMSPACE

While waiting for the Web's Virtual Reality Modeling Language (VRML) to become available for the personal computer, I became interested in three-dimensional action games that have shareware level editors. Numerous editors have appeared on the Net, so in addition to simply being able to experience the original game, people can edit and create their own spaces or levels, and, if the game is multi-player, experience them with other players.

Although other games followed, *Doom* was my first attempt at creating levels. *Doom* is a multiplayer, action-adventure game that originated on the Internet as shareware. Unlike *Myst*, for example, which is a series of hot-linked dissolving screens, *Doom* involves travel through a real three-dimensional environment and makes it possibile for up to four players to experience the space interactively. Although limited in travel to the second dimension, *Doom*'s relative speed and its wide availability make it the program closest to virtual reality that many people can afford to enjoy.

The views shown here represent the painting modeled in DoomCad and DCK 2.2 (Doom Construction Kit). The painting forms are developed as volumes, with the largest of these becoming the open court. The volumes step down in elevation from north to south. The smaller plan spaces become deep light-wells, illuminated by strobing light, open to the sky. Windows and portals provide views across and through the space.

The next generation of games with more complex graphics engines will have fully three-dimensional spaces, and improved artificial intelligence. To further promote these games, companies are releasing many of them with their own editors, and, in combination with Internet multiplayer capabilities, home-brewed levels may very well rival VRML chat spaces.

Screen snapshots

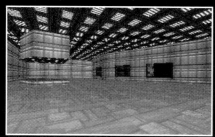

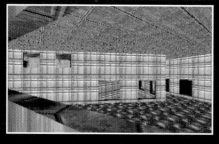

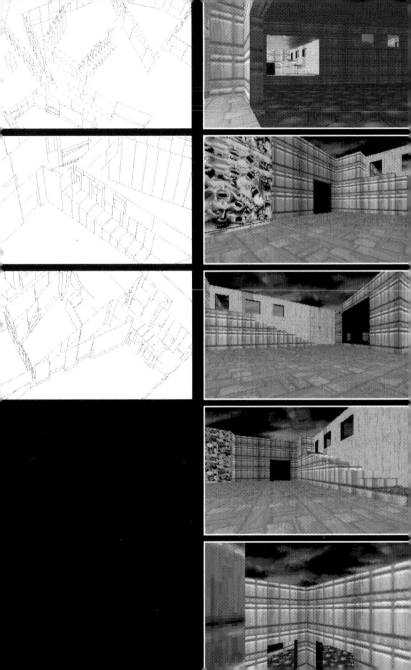

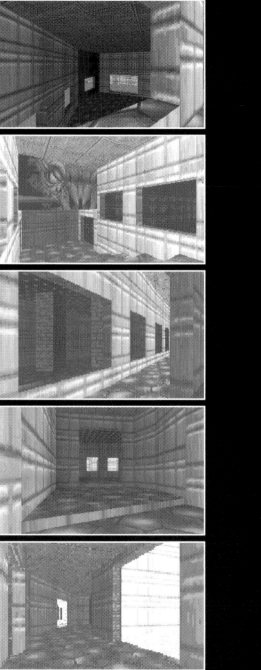

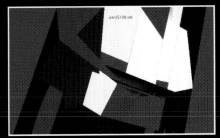

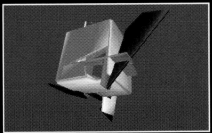

ZenLux Estates

Duncan Brown

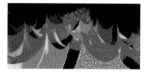

ZenLux portfolio

[Duneray Gallery] [Fourteenth Street Mall] [Irving Place Apartment] [Rapid Prototyping Models]

Architecture is the social practice of making spaces. While generating spaces on the computer is a reclusive activity, a virtual architecture achieves its public presence on the Web. The digital allows architecture, in a more encompassing sense, to preempt our increasingly closed and commodity-laden spatial existence. The possibility of meaningful virtual community is clearly present and genuinely occupiable electronic spaces are being created. Architects ought to be trailblazing the frontier for a new heroic architecture, almost as though it were a new continent.

The physical boundaries and limitations that had existed between many spatial mediums become fluid within the realm of the computer, and architects find themselves less isolated and more dispersed within a variety of other fields. The process-oriented transformational techniques of the 1980s have found direct application by utilizing the computer's inherent capabilities. Compositional strategies are being developed as a variant of genetic modeling and for the presentation of other data—stock information or musical sounds, for example.

VRML is the multiplatform language that allows for the experience and distribution of spaces on the Web—public architecture in cyberspace. Sadly, most Web-worlds seem to land somewhere between Colonial Williamsburg and Levittown. Architects can reach beyond this application of a pattern language into new territory. Web documents can serve as the basis for real-world construction. The tools exist for the virtual practice; it is just a matter of their application.

Even before the inception of DuneRay, my intention was the transmission of dynamic spatial realms and their practical realization. As access speeds increase and the applications improve, hopefully, the combative nature of the gamers and the social character of the MUDs will be resolved into a spatially literate online community with an active and participatory role in the real world.

What began as a consideration of a graphic and its marginal relationship to architecture, with DuneRay and the painting-transformation, has developed into an exploration of the parallel relationship between electronic and real space. ZenLux is an investigation of architecture continuing in cyberspace, where the virtual practice is understood as an integrated component of the craft of spatial construction.

Previous—Zenlux VRML models. Opposite—Web page screen snapshots

ZenLux

- ZenLux : VRML Worlds
- ZenLux : Text and Images
- DuneRay : Text and Images
- Resources : VRML, Editors, Media
- SITES : SITES Magazine

Corporate Profile Correspondence

Projects

- Folded Form : Broken
- Edited Spaces : DoomSpace
- Programmed Building : SDC
- Apartment : Irving Place
- Rapid Prototyping : Stereolithography
- Mall : Fourteenth Street

Back to the ZenLux homepage

ZenLux

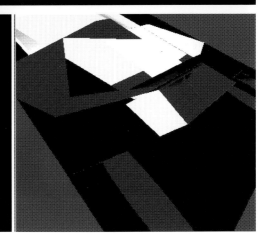

- ZenLuxVRML
- ZenLuxHTML
- ZenLuxInfo
- DuneRay
- ZenLuxMail
- SITESOnLine
- Resources

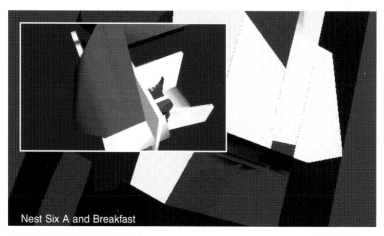

Nest Six A and Breakfast

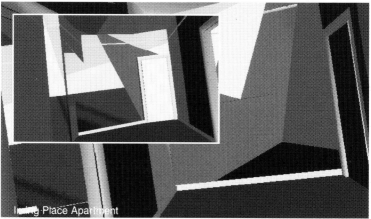

Living Place Apartment

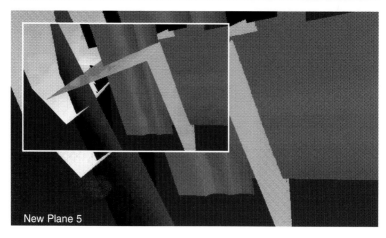

New Plane 5

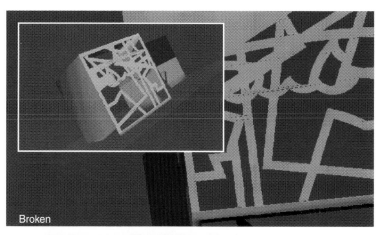

Broken

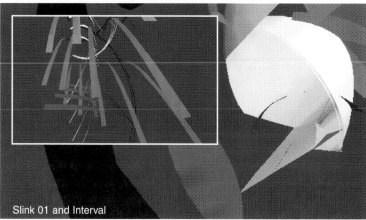

Slink 01 and Interval

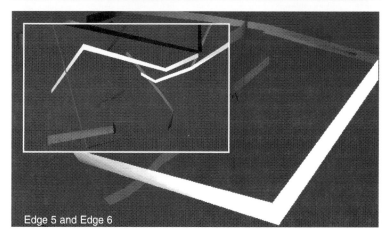

Edge 5 and Edge 6

THE VIRTUAL IDEA OF ZENLUX—DENNIS DOLLENS

Note: When DuneRay and ZenLux are italicized, the names refer to published books; when either is in roman type, it refers to the respective project.

 Early sections of *ZenLux*, called DuneRay, may be thought of in relation to cellular replication and manipulation: a surface, a line, a plane, or a series of each is taken from a section of a painting and reanimated, then bred into new forms, their structures rearranged without pictorial likeness to the original work, effectually reactivating geometries trapped in the inert media of old paint. In this experiment, Duncan Brown confronts the flat pictorial space of Western painting from within the computer and extracts possibilities for analyzing complex two-dimensional digital space as well as three-dimensional experimental and habitable space. As it appears in *ZenLux*, Brown's overall project thus becomes a primer for considering and designing three-dimensional forms from two dimensional images. In effect, DuneRay is a case study in the electronic manipulation of Juan Gris's 1914 Cubist painting *Breakfast* (p.4), where the painting is enlisted arbitrarily (any other image might have been substituted) to engender spatial transformations fragmented in virtual, then built, reality.

DuneRay picks up an unexplored trail of classic modernism and blasts it into electronic space while still breathing new life into the structure of Gris's experiment. The electronic transformation of pictorial line and surface (two-dimensions) into extruded form (three-dimensions) and eventually into models and building projects places ZenLux on a shifting edge of design innovation. Brown's methods signal one starting point for electronic architecture: structures developed from digitally reordered images that are manipulated using VRML, animation, CAD, graphic editors, and other electronic programming. ZenLux even seems to be nearing self-mutating or reader/user-mutated forms that have the potential (currently being investigated) to integrate artificial life and/or game architecture. Still, none of these methods or potential methods ignores traditional architectural practice; on the contrary, in Brown's work, projection, extrusion, rotation, and folding are critical praxes.

DuneRay was born between 1984 and 1991 in Duncan Brown's experimental "Painting Project." First, manipulating a postcard image of *Breakfast* (p.4), he disrupted the painting's surface through projection; later he cut and folded Gris's image, transforming it into a three-dimensional object. This experiment in turn led the architect, using MicroStation software, to approximate the folded structure electronically. After digitalization, the painting took on a new and different life as its continuous surface became discontinuous, a shifting template for warping, folding, and extruding. Brown's maneuvers with form and line traced a new architectural trajectory in architectural space and design. Among the many potential and realized experiments along this trajectory is DuneRay itself.[1] And among the many potential interpretations of DuneRay is the view of it as an architectural "noise" generator, scrambling *Breakfast's* flat, antique surface and two-dimensional forms into virtual space and Web presence. Brown dislocated and freed the painting from its history and inserted it into an electronic reality where it engenders thousands of images and structures. Pages 6 and 7, titled "Operations," offer a grammar of shapes and transformations illustrating some of the geometric operations that comprise DuneRay.

Abstracting and/or distorting fragments of Gris's painting, Brown created schematic likenesses of the original and then further digitally manipulated these with the intention, among other things, of extracting from DuneRay a graphic-novel, and, in his words, a "source of extra-architectural origin, simultaneously allowing for reflection on existing spatial hierarchies while serving to dislocate and expand current spatial ideas." Brown has further stated that "all the compositions illustrated are projected, generated, or folded from line sequences inherent in the painting."[2] From his parasitic raid on the painting, the architect has demonstrated that analog images hold the potential for electronic reanimation and that such reanimation then may lead to architecture.

In one sense, the limited edition, graphic-novel DuneRay[3] was the first manifestation of architecture, albeit a paper architecture, to come out of Brown's ongoing project, even though it retained a linear, cinematographic air, a comic-book likeness, and no text. The graphic-novel was created from virtual three-dimensional structures in electronic space (hence architecture), while its graphic framing produced narrative structures akin to fictional space. Here, for example, is a space in William Gibson's *Neuromancer:*

> . . . the paneled room folded itself through a dozen impossible angles, tumbling away into cyberspace like an origami crane.[4]

Doesn't that sound the way much of *DuneRay* looks (pp. 8-13)? *DuneRay* visually produced a narrative comparable to Gibson's sentence, but in a nonverbal roll of forms. And *DuneRay's* panels script a series of other pictorial scenarios that are simultaneously spatial explorations. As I read *DuneRay* in its silent, novelistic mode, I see its images as a spatial sequence that stems from and blurs (by integration) the boundaries of other twentieth-century art forms—painting and cinema—as well as, if more prosaically, comic books and science fiction, and, more importantly, architecture and electronics.

Further manipulated in MicroStation and printed as drawings or later as stereolithographic models, DuneRay quickly shed all likeness to Gris's work. Now, distinct from the painting that challenged early twentieth-century optical sequencing, DuneRay's images immediately challenge and/or spark our late twentieth-century spatial imagination. Assessing the potential power of such images, we can see that they manifest physical space relevant to open, urban contexts

(Cubital Models, pp. 34-39), domestic interiors ("Irving Place Apartment," pp. 24-27), and buildings ("14th Street Mall" pp. 20-23 and the "Scottish Design Center," pp. 40-45), as well as to Web and virtual spaces ("Broken" pp. 28-33 and "DoomSpace," pp. 46-49). Somewhere in this lineage Brown's conceptualization of the project required a splitting of typologies—not a surgical split, but a kind of slow morphing where early novelistic and cinematographic concerns of DuneRay are subsumed although not totally replaced by those of later gaming or competition programs—so Brown devised a bi-level organization, which is where his new rubric, ZenLux, comes into play.[5]

ZenLux continually reinvents and shifts its starting points as it revisits early forms. For example, the lessons from folding a continuous, three-dimensional surface out of the original postcard were followed, logically, by the series of forms typified by "Nest 8" (p. 8), but the same lessons were again recently applied in a more stealthlike way, resulting in the Web version of "Broken" as an animated, continuous-surface, folding form (p. 28). This kind of chronological lapse gives Brown the freedom to view the warps that time inherently applies and to go back to his various starts for different forms and new experiments. In this way the individual experiments mark or tag components of DuneRay or ZenLux as parts of a loose but mutually related system; the experiments also make viewers potentially able to mimic early experiments and impose *ZenLux* onto their own tectonic interests as a system mnemonic. *ZenLux* becomes a sort of dispersed hyperarchitecture.[6]

Recently, I found that by copying Brown's initial experiment I was better able to understand the three-dimensional forms in his series around "Nest 8" and that those forms apply and reapply throughout the evolution of DuneRay into ZenLux. By taking a scanned, computer print of *Breakfast* and slitting it along selected junctures of its pictured forms, and then folding and torquing those tab-like slits, finally attaching them to the now warped underside of the image, I was able to reproduce a DuneRay seed. Besides having the proto-electronic DuneRay element, the resulting physical model provided an extremely clear form whose complex folds aptly illustrate the spatial intricacy of its electronic counterparts. After showing this formal plagiarism to Brown, I learned an important developmental aspect of his project: some such structures were unstable "in a figurative, formal sense as well as literally," Brown noted, and he had responded to this problematic instability by inserting cubic or cruciform armatures. Indeed, my "FauxRay" was an unstable, shaky three-dimesional blob that needed structural stabilization. Still, besides opening a tiny window on the process of how structure comes into play in Brown's folded and extruded architecture, the expenditure of an hour or so in making a model paid off in my learned ability to play and spin an analog form that carried information and bore an uncanny relationship to its electronic progeny. Furthermore, having built a model, I could see clearly what a transferable, didactic tool it was and how ideal an introduction to some concepts of electronic architecture it is for students.

The paper model also clarified Brown's development of several projects that straddle obscure points of transformation between DuneRay and ZenLux, for example, the modeling of an interior apartment space whose antecedents predate DuneRay's electronic images and can be traced to the early postcard and electronic fold-models. And his original paper model (top, left: p. 36) also marks the physical track leading to Brown's Cubital models and "Broken" (pp. 28-33), while in hindsight they appear to signal how Brown abstracted, positioned, and recycled *Breakfast* in order to generate actual, buildable space—how the virtual DuneRay was conceptualized and made physical. This process is further articulated and refined in "Broken," where, in addition to illustrations and models, a brief prose description may be read as an abstract "How-to." The description along with "Operations" (pp. 6-7) and the generative developments illustrated in "Armatures" (pp. 62-63), are effectually a procedural documentation of *ZenLux* and can be read and assembled almost as a Chomskylike shape grammar.

After the paper models, Brown used the computer to fold *Breakfast*'s image into boxes, then used the boxes as a template to guide the interior painting of his former New York apartment into a DuneRay sequence (pp.24-27). What was interesting in this experiment is how effectively the apartment mirrored electronic and gamelike spaces while also relating to prosaic interior architecture and, of course, *Breakfast* itself. Interesting too, the apartment predated Brown's current manipulation of game spaces in *DoomSpace* (pp. 46-49). Yet, in an ironic turn, the apartment was a device for perceptually shifting and distorting existing right angles, wall planes, and architectural hierarchies, while the game's angular spaces are rigidly held and articulated within an enforced hierarchy of points and lines in an established universe (where points are pivotal spots for straight lines needed "to walk/run" and navigate the game's corridors). Enigmatically, the "dumb" apartment was a far more advanced "game" than its "smart" electronic counterparts. In the actual apartment, interior isomorphic junctures were perceptually reordered, optically transforming the painted walls into a "game" field that forced the viewer into an internal relationship with DuneRay and the existing architecture (much the way that DuneRay originally forced itself onto *Breakfast*). In Brown's apartment, one was prisoner of DuneRay. And, as Brown erected life-size "Broken" constructions in these same rooms (pp. 32-33, Web pages, top p.53), a cubic "Broken" became a gamelike avatar, physically obscuring the painted space even while the painted space obscured the existing architectural space—a habitable interior set within an interior set—interlacing space into a cyclical self-referential, self-similar system that directed one's vision along channels akin to those available in VR.

The apartment was DuneRay/ZenLux's first manifestation as a full-scale architectural transformation. Both existing apartment and existing painting were subverted into the structural background and made to bear Brown's overwriting—while Brown inhabited one and was enveloped by the other. Such overwriting moved from appropriating *Breakfast* to appropriating a portion of a building and in the future will likely move to appropriating exterior space. An aggressive hyperarchitecture. In addition to the shifting geometries and the optical plays, when you sat in Brown's apartment or sat in the "Broken" avatars in the apartment, you were enveloped in a sort of riddle or puzzle—where were you? In *Breakfast*? In *Doom* space? In the first architecture of VRML? In a painting? Truth is, you were in *trompe l'oeil*; but the important event was that you were moved out of the space of a monitor. So, as in the early stages of DuneRay, the viewer was transported into a private world—in this case, of visual puns and spatial subversion—where Brown (and the viewer) explored the "extra-architectural." Things really weren't what they appeared.

As with many mutations, the project's relationships to its original seed became less and less apparent as new forms evolved. And while *Breakfast* permeates all of DuneRay, the painting is only glimpsed in later and ongoing components of ZenLux. (Two schematic views of the painting appear on page16.) In the two years or so since I began this text, continual experimental mutations have lead Brown in several directions. He has entered and exited a modeling phase using Cubital's rapid prototyping stereolithography where he produced a series of three-dimensional objects directly from computer files. These small, hardened resin pieces illustrate some of the various potential spaces that can be directly realized through his spatial manipulations. To date, he has completed three models. The first (p. 34) explored the potentials of right angles, planar surfaces, and cubic volumes; the second (p. 35) explored the potentials of a hollow cube whose sides were slashed, including incisions that crossed the 90° wall intersections; while the third and most complex (pp. 37-39) explored warped surfaces, curves, and intersecting arcs in what might be realized as a small park or plaza. Besides the obvious usefulness of modeling directly from software, Brown's stereolithography reinforces the didactic potential of his design process, demonstrating how ZenLux's abstract and sometimes arbitrary imaging leads not to arbitrary space but, rather, to designed electronic spaces that can be extracted physically from virtual space.

Several of Brown's other projects oscillate between DuneRay and ZenLux. One, the "14th Street Mall" (pp. 20-23), a structure for a site next to New York's 4th Avenue, was configured through forms first projected from *Breakfast*, then given a program, and finally articulated in relation to its surroundings. Only by knowing its derivation can one link the mall's rectangular elements to Gris. Yet, beyond its form and generation, this plan for a large building takes on significance to ZenLux as an urban-scale extension, illustrating for the first time that "real" architecture is one of Brown's objectives.

If the forms of the "14th Street Mall" are schematic, a study in resolving program, site, and plan—with *Breakfast* then developing extrusions and volumes—Brown's next building project, a competition entry for the "Scottish

Design Center" (pp. 40-45), was a fully realized proposal for an inner-city site. While the entry stems from DuneRay, the added mutation of a commercial project's necessary program obscures some of the more radical forms seen in other DuneRay projects. Yet, even with its real-world restrictions, the design center is fully linked to *Breakfast*. Brown has stated that "I introduced three type models from the painting—representative of three geometric orders. The models underwent . . . transformation relative to each other and in response to general programmatic and contextual influences." The three resulting forms—crystalline blocks as offices, cylinder as IMAX theater, and parabolic, concrete vaults as design showrooms—are the only parts of ZenLux that Brown has pushed into such programmatic restrictions (so far), and they illustrate how flexible he has kept ZenLux as a working system. The "Scottish Design Center" not only responds to its site, but does so by observing historic materials and scale, pedestrian and vehicular traffic, as well as landscaping. Thus, we have an example of ZenLux in a context radically different from that of its electronic homeland.

While the "Scottish Design Center" functions within an existing urban chaos, "ZenLux Estates" (pp. 14-19) creates its own: a clear, mazelike, acrylic model that falls somewhere in Brown's work between the Cubital models and his retrofitting the uncharted corridors of *Doom*. The Estates model originates from electronically plotted drawings describing *Breakfast*'s shortest horizontal and vertical lines (top p. 16). It is a set piece—related to a short story and computer graphics (p. 15)—that you "enter" at a conceptual point that is the extreme opposite of the conceptual point you use, metaphorically, to enter, say, the "Scottish Design Center." Both worlds, cyber and analog, are playing off (and on) one another in a lightly subversive continuation of ZenLux as a game, as a strategy, as a storyboard, and specifically as a planning conundrum (one with clear relations to the interior manipulations of Brown's former apartment). The evolution toward space as playing field, space as game, and architecture as shell and container of the "event" seems to balance Brown's real-world moves toward projects represented by the "Scottish Design Center."

Viewed from the perspective of "ZenLux Estates," ZenLux's architectural 'gaming' begins to schematically paint the possibility of a VR architecture. Looking at "ZenLux Estates" and the "Apartment" interior as sample architectural environments and imbuing "Broken" with avatarlike qualities, we can envision ZenLux's development as movement toward new transformation protocols, which in turn lead to the construction of electronic architecture—real and virtual.

Brown has quoted Andrew Ross: "Making our knowledge about technoculture into something like a hacker's knowledge, capable of penetrating existing systems of rationality that might otherwise be seen as infallible; a hacker's knowledge, capable of reskilling and, therefore, of rewriting the cultural programs and reprogramming the social values that make room for new technologies."[7] Using this quotation in relation to strategies informing ZenLux, Brown has, as with

Breakfast, appropriated another's work for purposes of attaching and mutating. Additionally, Brown's redeployment of Ross's terms "reskilling," "rewriting," and "reprogramming," along with the larger appropriation of "hacker" as metaphor, is in itself an act of hypertext.[8] Brown is transforming his knowledge of electronics and architecture, like a hacker's knowledge, into broad-based appropriation—of painting, electronics, architecture, *Doom*, Ross, etc., etc.—and transforming that appropriation into the idea of electronic open design and architectural generation.

By now it must seem clear to you that ZenLux is a VI (Virtual Idea): a self-similar, hacked referent—a circular or spiraling system that appropriates things, forces them to mutate, changes their scale, and places them in proximate but not necessarily compatible projects. As ZenLux grows, its hacked-together complexion becomes more and more identifiable as Duncan Brown's product, and this book is the first guide to understanding, appropriating, and redeploying it. *ZenLux* may seem an exasperating hunk of disparate workings, a disunit of seemingly disjunctive ideas and subsystems, that is, until you deploy it. Then it's lightspeed.

Notes

1. Sections of earlier versions were published in SITES 24, SITES 26, and *New York: Nomadic Design*. The first exhibition took place at the Kohn Pedersen Fox Gallery (New York) in November 1993 and was followed by an exhibition at Columbia University's School of Architecture, February-March 1994. Portions appeared electronically from May 1994 to May 1995 on SITES ONLINE BBS.

2. Duncan Brown, SITES 24 (New York: Lumen, 1992): 60.

3. *DuneRay*, Graphic Novel Artist's Book, produced in an edition of 100, 1993.

4. William Gibson, *Neuromancer* (New York: Ace Books, 1984): 174.

5. The names DuneRay and ZenLux are difficult to account for fully, so I asked Brown to write a couple of paragraphs that explain them. Here, slightly edited, is his e-mail response to my request. "At the time I was working on what became DuneRay . . . I was looking for something that was about work or making, was related to me, where I came from, and had a sort of science-fiction/comic book ring to it. Dounreay was the name of the site of the nuclear power plant in the north of Scotland where my father worked and where our family lived. It was one of those reactors housed in a big sphere—quite a striking profile on the rugged coastline—something in the mind's eye-man/nature-power, fusion, fission. I changed the spelling to make it more phonetic and that reinforced the sci-fi theme . . .

"After DuneRay, I planned to do a little faux-monograph in ashcan format, taking the models and assigning real programs and locations to them. . . . At the time many corporations were appearing with names of two-syllable words like Chembank or Netscape. ZenLux came into being when I was crossing Park Avenue South on Seventeenth and looked up and realized that the Pan Am building had changed to the MetLife building. ZenLux was there by the time I had crossed the road; I was just rhyming things in my head. What does it mean? The luxury of nothing, perhaps appropriate for real spaces in the digital realm?"

6. Hyperarchitecture. This is my homegrown definition: The creation of architecture in an electronic realm where seams of creation disappear and where starting points may be extruded from nontraditional objects in an experimental process relying on the power of electronics to create, transform, grow, modify, and link media and/or text in a nonsequential, noncartesian manner.

7. Andrew Ross, *Strange Weather: Culture: Science, and Technology in the Age of Limits* (New York: Verso, 1991).

8. Hypertext. "An electronically created document providing links and paths connecting blocks of text and/or graphics that branch and allow the reader to manipulate the document in a nonsequential manner. . . . By giving users multiple paths to follow, hypertext also creates individual readings with no definitive text." George P. Landow, *Hypertext: The Convergence of Contemporary Critical Theory and Technology* (Baltimore: The Johns Hopkins Press, 1992).

SELECTED REFERENCES

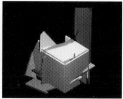

Armatures

FICTION

Amis, Martin. *London Fields*. New York: Vintage International, 1991.
Ballard, J.G. *The Atrocity Exhibition*. San Francisco: Re/Search Publications, 1990.
— *"the lost symmetry of the blastosphere"*
Bear, Greg. *Blood Music*. New York: Ace Books, 1986.
Burroughs, William. *Naked Lunch*. New York: Grove Press, 1959.
Gibson, William. *Neuromancer*. New York: Ace Books, 1984.
Howe, Susan. *The Europe of Trusts*. Los Angeles: Sun & Moon, 1990.
Perec, Georges. *Life: A User's Manual*. Trans. David Bellos. Lincoln, Mass:
    David R. Godine, 1988.
Robinson, Marilynne. *Housekeeping*. New York: Bantam, 1982.
— *"A house should have a compass and a keel."*
Stephenson, Neal. *Snow Crash*. New York: Bantam, 1992.
Winterson, Jeanette. *Sexing the Cherry*. New York: Vintage International, 1991.

NONFICTION

Bukatman, Scott. *Terminal Identity: The Virtual Subject in Postmodern Science
    Fiction*. Durham and London: Duke University Press, 1993.
— *the after the fact theoretical text for DuneRay.*
Debord, Guy. *Society of the Spectacle and Other Films*. Trans. Ken Sanborn and
    Richard Parry. London: Rebel Press, 1992.
Gutman, Robert. *Architectural Practice: A Critical View*. New York: Princeton
    Architectural Press, 1988.
Illich, Ivan. *Medical Nemesis: The Expropriation of Health*. New York: Pantheon,1976
— *architecture is suffering from the equivalent of physician-induced disease.*
Kelly, Kevin. *Out of Control: The Rise of Neo-Biological Civilization*. New York:
    Addison-Wesley Publishing Company, 1994— *"the Nine Laws of God."*
Ross, Andrew. *Strange Weather: Culture, Science, and Technology in the Age of
    Limits*. New York: Verso, 1991.
Sturrock, John, ed. *Structuralism and Since: From Levi-Strauss to Derrida*. New
    York: Oxford University Press, 1979.
Virilio, Paul. *The Aesthetics of Disappearance*. Trans. Philip Beitchman. New York:
    Semiotext(e), 1991— *"architecture is no longer in architecture, but in geometry;. . ."*

ARTICLES

Eisenman, Peter. "The End of the Classical, the End of the Beginning, the End
    of the End," *Perspecta* 21 (Summer 1984): 154-173.
Haraway, Donna. "A Cyborg Manifesto: Science, Technology, and Socialist-Feminism
    in the Late Twentieth Century," *Simians, Cyborgs, and Women: The Reinvention of
    Nature*. New York: Routledge, 1991.
— *"It means both building and destroying machines, identities, categories,
    relationships, spaces, stories."*
Krauss, Rosalind. "Sculpture in the Expanded Field," *Postmodern Culture*. Ed.
    Hal Foster. London and Sydney: Pluto Press, 1985: 31-42.

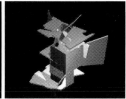

Tschumi, Bernard. "Illustrated Index: Themes from the Manhattan Transcripts,"
    AA Files. London: The Architectural Association, 1983: 65-74.
    —*classification . . . transformation . . . combination . . .*
Moneo, Rafael. "The Work of John Hedjuk or the Passion to Teach," *Lotus
    International* 11: 64-81.
    —*my first exposure to an architectural interpretation of Juan Gris.*

COMICS
Adamov and Cothias. "The Waters of Dead Moon." *Heavy Metal*. New York: HM
    Communications. May and September 1990, September 1991, September 1992.
    —*some of the Dead Moon landscapes were inspiration for DuneRay frames.*
Chaykin, Howard. *American Flagg!*—*Hard Times*, Evanston, IL.: First Comics, 1983.
McFarlane, Todd *Spawn*. Westlake Village, CA: Image/ Malibu Comics, 1992.
Miller, Frank. "Sin City," *Dark Horse Presents*. Milwaukie. OR.: Dark Horse
    Comics, 1991. (Thirteen-issue series appeared in 1991-1992.)
Miller, Frank, with Klaus Janson and Lynn Varley. *Batman—The Dark Knight Returns*.
    New York: DC Comics, 1986. (Four-issue series appeared in 1986.)
    —*this was the series that revitalized my interest in comics.*

MOVIES—http://us.imdb.com/Movies/search.html
Akira. Katsuhiro Otomo, 1988. 124 mins.
Alphaville. Jean-Luc Godard, 1965. 100 mins.
Altered States. Ken Russell, 1980, 102 mins.
Blade Runner. Ridley Scott, 1982. 118 mins.
Fahrenheit 451. Francois Truffaut, 1967. 111 mins.
The Grifters. Stephen Frears, 1990, 119 mins.
Jacob's Ladder. Adrian Lyne, 1990, 115 mins.
Lady from Shanghai. Orson Welles, 1948, 87 mins.
Night and the City. Jules Dassin, 1950, 95 mins.
North by Northwest. Alfred Hitchcock, 1959, 136 mins.
Paris, Texas. Wim Wenders,1984, 150 mins.
The Player. Robert Altman, 1992, mins.
Stalker. Andrei Tarkovsky, 1979. 160 mins.
Terminator 2. James Cameron, 1991. 137 mins.
Total Recall. Paul Verhoeven, 1990. 109 mins.
Until the End of the World. Wim Wenders, 1991, 179 mins.
Videodrome. David Cronenberg, 1982. 90 mins.
A Zed and Two Noughts. Peter Greenaway, 1985, 116 mins.

VRML—http://www.lightside.com/~dani/cgi/VRML-index.html
Ames, Andrea L., David R. Nadeau, and John L. Moreland. *The VRML
    Sourcebook*. New York: John Wiley and Sons, 1996.
Pesce, Mark. *VRML-Browsing and Building Cyberspace*. Indianapolis:
    New Riders, 1995.

TECHNICAL INFORMATION

HARDWARE

1982   Sinclair ZX Spectrum (sold late 1980s)
1992   Gateway 2000 486 DX33 with 8MB RAM (sold Spring 1996)
       • 8MB RAM added Fall 1994
       • Sound card added Spring 1995
1993   Hewlett Packard IIP Plus (sold Spring 1995)
       Canon BJC 600 (sold Spring 1995)
1994   Colorado Trakker 250 Tape Back-up
       US Robotics Sportster 14,400 Fax/Modem
1995   Snappy Video Snapshot (sold Summer 1996)
       Backpack Quad Speed CD-ROM (sold Winter 1995)
       Hewlett Packard LaserJet 5P
       Dell Dimension XPS P133c

SOFTWARE

Desktop Publishing
Adobe Photoshop 2.5
GrabIt Professional 5.0
LViewPro
Quark Xpress 3.32
Snappy

CAD
Microstation 5.0
3D Studio (animation on pp. 6-7, 27)

Game Editors
DCK 2.2—*Doom*
DoomCad 5.1—*Doom*
Devil—*Descent*

VRML
Fountain—Scene builder
Live 3D—Browser
Pioneer—Scene builder
Wcvt2pov—File convertor
WebFx—Browser

WETWARE

The Cubital models were created at Toledo Molding and Die in Toledo, Ohio.

The ZenLux acrylic model was built by Kennedy Fabrications in New York.

Dan Howell took the photographs of the Irving Place apartment and the ZenLux model.

Thanks to my family and friends in Manchester, New York, and San Francisco.

Special thanks to Dennis Dollens for his enthusiastic support and ongoing counsel.